Christmas

YVONNE DE SIKE

Christmas

HACHETTE
Illustrated

Contents

The Three Kings, Epiphany, 19th century. Painting.

Private collection, Slovenia.

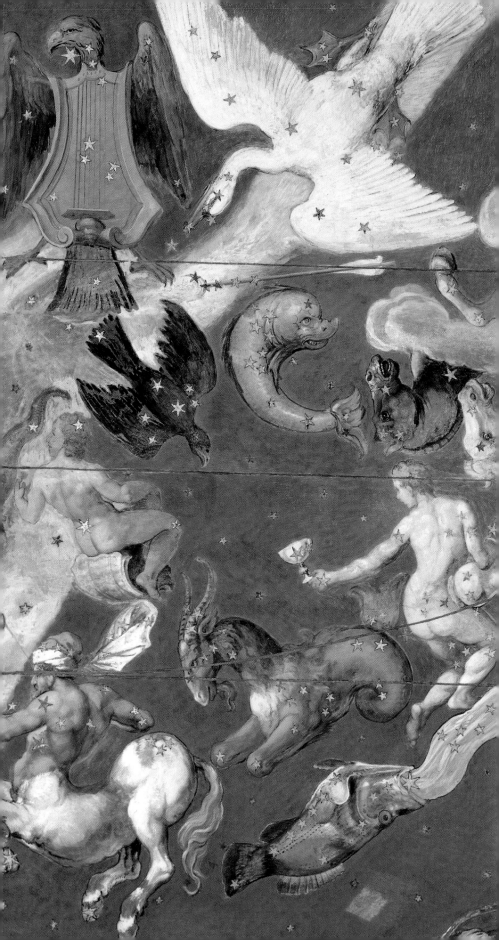

MEASURING TIME

W e celebrate Christmas on 25 December,
but this date was only fixed some 350 years
after the Birth of Jesus. To find out why,
we have to go back thousands of years to the Babylonian
astronomer-scribes, who were the first to codify the
bewildering mass of information contained in the
vast skies above them, and arrive at a workable calendar
system.

As Planet Earth, our spaceship, travels on its course
towards the infinite, it has been harnessed to the solar
system for thousands of millions of years. It turns
untiringly on its own axis, from west to east, revealing in
turn different parts of itself to the Sun. The Sun is the star
which provides our source of light and life. The Earth's
rotation, which takes 23 hours, 56 minutes and 4 seconds
to complete, transforms day into night and makes it seem
as though the Sun moves every day from the east, where it
rises, to the west, where it sets. At the same time, the Earth
turns round the Sun in 365 days, 5 hours, 148 minutes and

*G de Vecchi and
R da Regio, Zodiac
and Constellations,
15th century. Palazzo
Farnese, Italy.*

7

14 seconds. The Earth's axis of rotation, an imaginary line joining the North and South Poles and pointing at the North Star, has an inclination of 23.5°. As a result, the Earth's two hemispheres face the Sun in succession; this alternation gives rise to the seasons and explains the origins of our rites and celebrations.

The first attempts to measure time were linked to the phases of the Moon. This was in remote antiquity. The arrival of a new Moon was a cause for wonder, prayers and

H *Kraemer*, Starry Sky on the Other Side of the Equator, *after a painting by* W *Kranz*, 1905.

rejoicing throughout the world. However, this satellite of Earth took 29.53059 days to complete one revolution, which made the 12 months of the lunar calendar about 11 days shorter than the solar year.

This disturbing shortfall stimulated all kinds of mathematical and astronomical ideas. The Babylonians, who insisted on staying with the lunar calendar, finally set up a system devised by the astronomer Meton around 432 BC. This used intercalary months which were added on every 19 years. Even today, with some minor differences, this remains the ritual calendar of the Jews and the Muslims.

The Egyptians abandoned the deceptive simplicity of the lunar month in favour of another means of measuring their year. They noticed that once a year Sirius, the brightest star in the Northern Hemisphere, rose at the same time as the Sun. This heliacal event, which took place in scorching heat in the middle of the flooding season on the Nile, became the beginning of the Egyptian year and an occasion for ceremonies to mark the creation of the world. This year lasted 365 days – 6 hours shorter than the solar year – and was adopted by Julius Caesar, who in 46 BC set up a new calendar, known as the Julian Calendar, of 365 days and 6 hours. He was obliged to preserve 1 January, which had been observed by the Romans since 153 BC.

The Julian Calendar survived for many centuries in Europe, and was used by Copernicus in the 16th century. However, it did not adequately take account of the length of the year, being 11 minutes longer than the solar year, and this threw it out of line with the solstices and equinoxes. In the second half of the 16th century, the spring equinox, an essential date for determining Easter, corresponded to 11 March. The need for reform was urgent, and Pope Gregory XIII took the necessary measures. In 1582, he decreed that 4 October would be directly followed by the 15th, to compensate for the discrepancy of 12 days. Since then, precise calculations have ensured that the Gregorian Calendar does not stray from the length of the solar year. However, this pontifical reform was not adopted everywhere. Because the innovation had come from Rome, Britain and the American colonies did not convert to it until 1752. The Orthodox Church, anxious to avoid falling subject to the Pope, still calculates the date of Easter according to the Julian Calendar, while some traditional-minded communities continue to celebrate Christmas and Epiphany using the old method, which gives them a discrepancy of 12 days.

Manuscript from Tübingen, Plan of the Celestial Bodies, with Elements from the Sphere of Michael Scotus, 15th century.

Denis the Little's Christian dating system

ntil the 6th century AD, the years were numbered *ab urbe condita*, counting from the foundation of Rome. The Greeks used the institution of the Olympic Games as their initial date, while the Jews used the date of the creation of the world according to the Bible. Pope John I became convinced that this method of dating was not good for developing loyalty among new converts. He asked a monk called Dionysius Exiguus, also known as Denis the Little, to organise a Christian chronology for the history of mankind that was founded on a major event of the new faith: the Birth of Christ. After making many calculations, the learned monk fixed the Birth of Christ at 25 December 753 AUC (*ab urbe condita*). Then he started the Christian year at 1 January 754 AUC, the day of the Roman New Year, which also matched the day the Infant Jesus was circumcised.

★ ★ ★

But Denis placed the Birth of Jesus 4 years after the death of King Herod, which contradicted the accounts given in the Gospels. Although the precise date of the Birth of Jesus remains unclear, it is known that Herod died in 750 AUC or 4 BC. According to the Gospels of Luke and Matthew, Jesus and Herod were alive at the same time: a *sine qua non* for the Massacre of the Innocents occurring after the Magi had returned to their own countries, and for the Holy Family's Flight into Egypt.

The Stella Nova and the Age of Pisces

s early as 1606, Kepler worked out in *De Stella Nova* that the star of Bethlehem was the result of a conjunction of the planets Mars, Jupiter and Saturn in Pisces. They stood in alignment as seen from Earth on 7 March, 7 BC, and created the impression of an enormous star: 'Great men are born at the time of such conjunctions,'

Kepler observed. Other learned men put forward other dates: 12 BC, corresponding to the passing of Halley's comet; 11 BC and also 4 BC, the date that the Capricorn Nova exploded. Since the Renaissance, astrologers have sought to establish a natal chart for Jesus with the beginning of the Age of Pisces coinciding with the Birth of Jesus. According to the calculations of Babylonian astronomers, an exceptional conjunction of several planets with the Moon and the Sun took place between February and March in 6 BC. This phenomenon could well correspond to the Biblical star. Meanwhile, the census which made Joseph and Mary leave their home, and was the reason why the inns were full, would have taken place around Passover in 6 BC.

H *Vorgtherr the Elder,* Two Astronomers Observing the Starry Sky, 1545. *Wood engraving.*

Decembre a xxxi iours
Et la lune xxx.
aint eloy
aint flauu
aint claudien
aint ambroise
aint barbe
aint nicholas
aint faur
ostre dame
aint eulalie
aint fulgen
aint valerien
aint auien
aint michaue
aint cyprien
aint maxime

Why We Celebrate Christmas on 25 December

In the first few centuries of Christianity, the Primitive Church paid little attention to the Birth of Jesus. It chiefly celebrated Easter, and Christ's Resurrection, the proof of redemption. Around 200 AD, Clement of Alexandria openly mocked those who tried to fix a reliable historical date for Easter; at the time it was said to occur on 19 April or 20 May. In about 243 AD, the bishop and martyr Cyprian claimed after mystical and symbolic calculations that the most favourable date was 28 March. The Creation of the World, when Light was separated from Darkness, seemed to correspond to the spring equinox, and since God had created the Sun and the Moon on the fourth day, it was logical to suppose that Christ, the Sun of Justice, was born on 28 March.

★ ★ ★

Even if these calculations seem fanciful to us, they reveal the concern of the early Fathers of the Church to identify Jesus with the ancient solar deities. On the bas-reliefs on

Calendar from a Book of Hours, The Month of December, 15th century. Illuminated manuscript. Museum of the Middle Ages, Cluny.

sarcophagi, paintings and mosaics from the early Christian period, the Sun and Moon are often shown next to the Cross, to express the divine (solar) and human (lunar) nature of Jesus, the Sun of Life. From this stemmed the unchanging principle of salvation for all eternity.

★ ★★

Around 330, when the new religion was made official by Constantine the Great, the Latin Churches decided to institute a special festival to celebrate the Birth of Jesus 'in the flesh'. After much wavering, they fixed the date at 25 December, without any documentary or Biblical backing. The choice of this date is generally seen as the fulfilment of a wish to make the Birth of Jesus correspond to other commemorative occasions, which were very popular in the Roman Empire. A grand celebration to honour the *Sol invictus*, the Sun Triumphant, had taken place at the winter solstice and, on the same date, the birth of Mithras, the Persian solar divinity, was celebrated. This was especially popular with the legionnaires, and since 275 AD, in the reign of Aurelian, the Emperor had been seen as the incarnation of Mithras. In addition, in the days leading up to the solstice, from 18 to 22 December, the people of Rome took part in celebrations, masquerades and ritual pantomimes to honour Saturn, the god of sowing (*satus* means sowing) and avatar of Cronus, the old god of agriculture. A week later, the first day of the calends of January was dedicated to Janus, the two-faced god and mythical king of Rome. At that time, the festival symbolised the passing from one year to the next, and to mark the occasion people showed their happiness by decorating their houses with ivy, branches of pine, laurel and olive. Presents, such as terracotta dolls and masks, were exchanged between family members, and everyone joined in songs calling for good health and the granting of their dearest wishes.

★ ★★

The Eastern Churches considered the Baptism of Christ, conducted by John the Baptist in the waters of the Jordan, to be the key date in Christianity. This divine apparition marked the first manifestation of the Trinity and also recognised the divine

origins of Jesus through His 'divine birth', and according to them took place on 6 January. From the 2nd century, the Eastern Christians, faced with choosing a date for the Birth of Christ, also opted for 6 January, which happily coincided with the birth dates of other gods from the Eastern Mediterranean. First of these was Tammuz, the Assyrian god of agriculture, who was born on that day some 3000 years earlier. Then there was Dionysus-Zagreus, who was assassinated by the Titans and was reborn each year on 6 January. Later, as Dionysus, he became the god of wine, the sacred drink of the gods, and was thought, like Orpheus, to be a precursor of the Saviour. During the night of 5–6 January, Egyptians celebrated the birthday of Aeon, the sun god, the offspring of Kore the Virgin. During their vigil, people sang songs and hymns to the sound of flutes; at dawn, before the first cock-crow, they went down into an underground cave to honour the divine child in his swaddling clothes, for, as Macrobius declared, 'on that day, the shortest of the year, the sun looks to some extent like a small child'.

Master Ermengaut,
The Breviary of
Love, January,
Janus, folio 57 verso,
13th–15th century.
Miniature. Royal
Library, Escurial.

Following two pages:
Cornelius Lucas,
The Months of
Lucas, January,
detail. Gobelins
tapestry, silk.
Château de Pau,
France.

So, on the same date, Christians of that time celebrated the Incarnation of Jesus, the true Sun, born of the Virgin in a cave in Bethlehem, and also His Baptism, the Arrival of the Magi, and the Marriage at Cana, where He changed water into wine. In this way, the Eastern Church celebrated four Epiphanies of Jesus, and four demonstrations of His true nature and powers. The cave in Bethelehem was also thought to have had a previous famous occupant: the young god Tammuz, the ancestor of Gilgamesh.

Roman art, Early Empire, Mithraic Relief with the Signs of the Zodiac. *Estense Gallery and Museum, Modena.*

According to gnostic traditions, most of the solar divinities were born of immaculate conceptions by celestial virgins. Several of these had endured a Passion, followed by death and descent into Hell, only to be reborn later. In addition to Tammuz and Mithras, the Phrygian god Attis was also born of a virgin, on 25 December. Other traditions maintain that Krishna, Buddha and Mohammed were born on the day of the winter solstice.

★ ★ ★

John Chrysostom, the renowned preacher of the Eastern Church, contrived to have the date of 25 December definitively adopted by the Christian community. The Council of Agde made it obligatory in 506, and in 529 Emperor Justinian declared the Nativity to be a public holiday. As the different peoples of Europe later became Christian, they began to celebrate Christmas on 25 December. Saint Patrick imposed this day in

Ireland in 461, Saint Augustine of Canterbury established it formally in England in 604, Saint Columban in Switzerland in 615 and Saint Boniface in Germany in about 754. In the 9th century, Saint Anskar converted the Scandinavians and established the Christmas festival there, while Cyril and Methodius brought both the Orthodox Church and literacy to the Slav countries. Shortly before 1000, Saint Adalbert converted the Magyars and established Christmas in Hungary. Because the date 25 December corresponded to that of ancient feasts in various pre-Christian mythologies, it was adopted without difficulty by the new converts to Christianity. For Anglo-Saxons, it was in the period around the solstice when they celebrated the god Woden (Odin) charging through the sky, carrying soldiers and others who died in the previous year to the world beyond. The tradition of this sad procession of the dead lives on in Europe through masking rituals and, elsewhere, the grotesque dances that were widespread in the Middle Ages. The Nativity, with its message of peace and light, deeply touched the Germanic peoples who, fearful of malign spirits roaming about at this time of year, established their own 'Twelve Wild Nights' as an alternative 12-day period between Christmas and Epiphany. Perhaps these 12 days – which Christians always celebrated with a great ritual fervour, full of bright lights and joyous merrymaking – corresponded to the discrepancy between the 12 solar months and the 12 lunar months. In so doing, they retained the memory of the lunar and solar calendars, and of their fusion.

Viking art, Priest of the Cult of Odin, *c 800. Bronze. State Historical Museum, Stockholm.*

★ ★ ★

The winter solstice was an occasion for enormous nocturnal drinking sessions among all the Nordic peoples who yearned for the 'rebirth' of the sun and an end to the icy conditions of winter. At that time, Odin, the principal god of Nordic mythology, came to the help of men in distress. Disguised as a benevolent old man, he fought against demons and the cold. Going under the name of Ullr or Yule, he was worshipped at the hearth ablaze with pine logs. He visited all the faithful on a sledge drawn by reindeer or swans.

THE NATIVITY:

STORIES, SONGS AND POEMS
FROM MANY CENTURIES

GOSPELS AND PROTEVANGELIUM

NATIVITIES

THE MAGI

THE SHEPHERDS

The major religions, like the great civilisations, are always the result of a happy cross-fertilisation of several cultures. Christianity was shaped in a region rich in traditions and philosophical systems, and

Previous page: Master of the Missal of Berthold, The Journey of the Magi, ms 710, folio 19 verso, 13th century. Miniature on gold ground. Pierpont Morgan Library, New York.

from its inception has integrated elements from the Egyptians, Jews, Zoroastrians, Greeks and Romans, and later from the Celts and the Germanic and Slav peoples. Christianity's singular nature and its universal appeal arise precisely from its capacity to assimilate these influences and provide new creative models for the imagination. Christmas is certainly the most striking example of this admirable syncretism. Even today, the festival has lost almost nothing of its long-established prestige. The mystery of God made man is not only a concept for theological speculation. Anchored in this image is the nostalgia of all peoples for the 'paradise' of an

original state, and the human sense of a renewal out of the heart of darkness. Lights, joy, feasts and prodigal behaviour always accompany the approach of the Nativity, and harmonise with the cosmic phenomena and solar cults so dear to mankind since the beginnings of time.

★ ★★

The Birth of Christ, 6th century. Marble relief. Byzantine Museum, Athens.

Two of the Evangelists, Mark and John, seem to have cared little for the way Jesus was born. They begin their story with His baptism in the Jordan. Mark mentions that Jesus came from Nazareth, in Galilee, where His mother, brothers and sisters still lived. John, describing the gathering together of the Apostles, confirms that the Messiah was the son of Joseph of Nazareth. But these Galilean origins, which were still referred to in the 4th century, were later played down in favour of making the birth of Jesus coincide with the ancient prophecies which told of the birth of a Messiah born of the house of David.

This inconsistency was resolved by the Gospels attributed to Luke and Matthew, which had the Child born in Bethlehem, because of the census imposed by the Romans, and provided Him with an illustrious genealogy. Historians of the New Testament freely admit that these prologues about the Nativity and childhood of Jesus were added later, when the Eastern Churches saw it as their duty to bring the new faith to the many Jews living in the Mediterranean region within the Asiatic and African borders of the Roman Empire.

Gofridus,
The Epiphany.
Capitals from the
choir of the Church
of Saint-Pierre,
Chauvigny,
12th century.

The 'Apochryphal' Gospels which, according to the writings of Athanasias of Alexandria, were arbitrarily excluded from the canon towards the end of the 4th century, go much further. They contain many details about the life of Christ, and these pervaded religious sentiment in the early Christian period. They supplied picturesque details of the Nativity, telling their readers about the cave, the ox and the ass, the presence of midwives, the crowns of the Magi, etc, and in the process a number of people emerged from their previous anonymity in the Gospels. The Apocrypha also provide the main details we have about Mary: her childhood, her life with Joachim and Ann, her parents, the Presentation in the Temple, and her everlasting virginity. The rich prose of the Apocrypha, with its profusion of touching details, had a great influence on the imaginations of medieval and Renaissance artists, who in turn created an abundance of sculptures, frescos, stained-glass windows, and mystical and profane literature. Their spirit lived on in the Mystery plays, pastorals and other theatrical presentations which, with their brief dialogues, powerful images and naive piety, for centuries provided a largely illiterate public with illustrations to the sacred texts. The Protevangelium of James, attributed to the apostle James the Less – the brother of Jesus according to the Gospels, or half-brother by his own account – provided information about the time before the birth of Jesus: the visit to Elizabeth, the mother of John the Baptist, how Joseph 'came from his building' and found Mary 'great with child', then about his doubts and the angel's confirmation of Mary's innocence. The revelations of James conclude with the death of Herod, and his own withdrawal into the desert to avoid the 'tumult' which then broke out. The *Story of Joseph the Carpenter* is the title of another Apocryphal text, of which two versions have survived, one in Coptic and one in Arabic. It describes the ancestry of Jesus 'in the flesh', His birth and a wealth of detail about His childhood, mainly inspired by the text of James. The second part, which describes the sickness and death of Joseph, makes the first mention of the veneration of Jesus's father 'in the flesh' by Coptic monks, according to the ancient rites of the cult of Osiris.

Erasmus Grasser,
The Birth of Christ,
1480. Relief in
painted wood.
Bavarian National
Museum, Munich.

After the Crusades and the decline of Latin kingdoms in the East, new themes were added to the tradition of the Nativity. The Eastern Churches had established a connection between Christmas and the creation of the world, and raised our biblical ancestors, Adam and Eve, to the status of 'saints'. They were celebrated on Christmas Eve to demonstrate the unity between the the creation of man and his redemption. This cult became very popular in the West. The pediments of several cathedrals contain images of our mythical parents, Adam and Eve, who, in their 'culpably' naked state, are depicted on either side of the fatal tree. In the 13th century, Jacobus de Voragine wrote his fabulous hagiography *The Golden Legend*. This introduced the West to the cult of Saint Nicholas who, in time, would become an important figure in popular observance of the Nativity.

Simone da Siena,
Birth of Christ,
1380–1420.
Collection of Songs.
Santa Croce, Florence.

Following two pages:
Andrea Mantegna,
The Adoration of
the Magi, 1464.
Tempera on wood.
Uffizi Gallery,
Florence.

And it came to pass in those days, that there went out a decree from Caesar Augustus, that all the world should be taxed. (And this taxing was first made when Cyrenius was governor of Syria.) And all went to be taxed, every one into his own city. And Joseph also went up from Galilee, out of the city of Nazareth, into Judaea, unto the city of David, which is called Bethlehem; (because he was of the house and lineage of David). To be taxed with Mary his espoused wife, being great with child.

And so it was that, while they were there, the days were accomplished that she should be delivered. And she brought forth her first-born son, and wrapped him in swaddling clothes, and laid him in a manger; because there was no room for them in the inn.

And there were in the same country shepherds abiding in the field, keeping watch over their flock by night. And, lo, the angel of the Lord came upon them, and the glory of the Lord shone round about them: and they were sore afraid. And the angel said unto them, Fear not: for, behold, I bring you good tidings of great joy, which shall be to all people. For unto you is born this day in the city of David a Saviour, which is Christ the Lord. And this shall be a sign unto you; Ye shall find the babe wrapped in swaddling clothes, lying in a manger. And suddenly there was with the angel a multitude of the heavenly host praising God, and saying, Glory to God in the highest, and on earth peace, good will towards men.

And it came to pass, as the angels were gone away from them into heaven, the shepherds said one to another, Let us now go even unto Bethlehem, and see this thing which is come to pass, which the Lord hath made known unto us. And they came with haste, and found Mary, and Joseph, and the babe lying in a manger. And when they had seen it, they made known abroad the saying which was told them concerning this child. And all they that heard it wondered at those things which were told them by the shepherds. But Mary kept all these things, and pondered them in her heart. And the shepherds returned, glorifying and praising God for all the things that they had heard and seen, as it was told unto them.

THE GOSPEL ACCORDING TO ST LUKE, 2, 1–20.

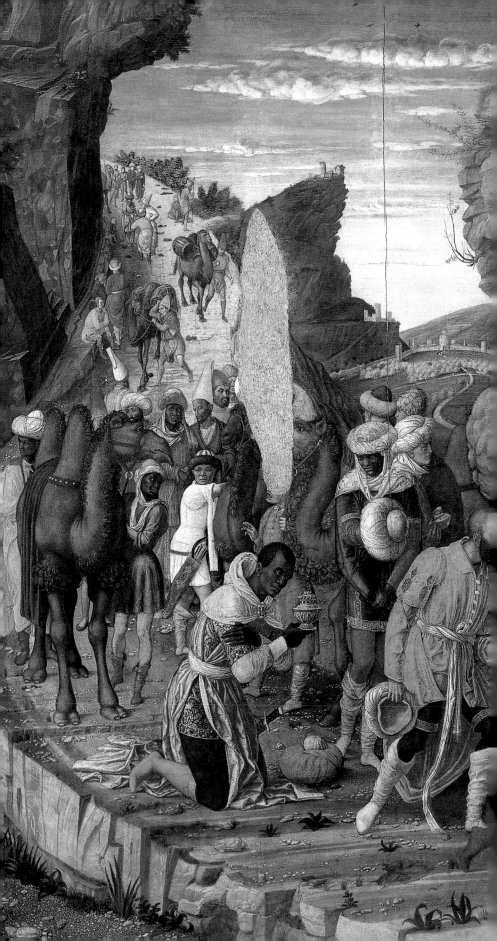

Now the birth of Jesus Christ was on this wise: When as his mother Mary was espoused to Joseph, before they came together, she was found with child of the Holy Ghost. Then Joseph her husband, being a just man, and not willing to make her a publick example, was minded to put her away privily. But while he thought on these things, behold, the angel of the Lord appeared unto him in a dream, saying,

Joseph, thou son of David, fear not to take unto thee Mary thy wife: for that which is conceived in her is of the Holy Ghost. And she shall bring forth a son, and thou shalt call his name JESUS: for he shall save his people from their sins. Now all this was done, that it might be fulfilled which was spoken of the Lord by the prophet, saying, Behold, a virgin shall be with child, and shall bring forth a son, and they shall call his name Emmanuel, which being interpreted is, God with us. Then Joseph being raised from sleep did as the angel of the Lord had bidden him, and took unto him his wife: And knew her not till she had brought forth her firstborn son: and he called his name JESUS.

Now when Jesus was born in Bethlehem of Judaea in the days of Herod the king, behold, there came wise men from the east to Jerusalem, Saying, Where is he that is born King of the Jews? for we have seen his star in the east, and are come to worship him. When Herod the king had heard these things, he was troubled, and all

Paolo di Giovanni Fei, Adoration of the Shepherds, 1372–1410. *Lindenau State Museum, Altenburg.*

Jerusalem with him. And when he had gathered all the chief priests and scribes of the people together, he demanded of them where Christ should be born. And they said unto him, In Bethlehem of Judaea: for thus it is written by the prophet. And thou Bethlehem, in the land of Juda, are not the least of the princes of Juda: for out of thee shall come a Governor, that shall rule my people Israel. Then Herod, when he had privily called the wise men, inquired of them diligently what time the star appeared. And he sent them to Bethlehem, and said, Go and search diligently for the young child; and when ye have found him, bring me word again, that I may come and worship him also. When they had heard the king, they departed; and lo, the star, which they saw in the east, went before them, till it came and stood over where the young child was. When they saw the star, they rejoiced with exceeding great joy. And when they were come into the house, they saw the young child with Mary his mother, and fell down, and worshipped him: and when they had opened their treasures, they presented unto him gifts; gold, and frankincense, and myrrh. And being warned of God in a dream that they should not return to Herod, they departed into their own country another way.

THE GOSPEL ACCORDING TO ST MATTHEW, 1, 18–25; 2, 1–12.

Paolo di Giovanni Fei, Adoration of the Kings, 1372–1410. Lindenau State Museum, Altenburg.

And I beheld a woman coming down from the hills, and she said unto me, Man, whither goest thou? And I said, I seek a midwife of the Hebrews.

And she answered and said unto me, Art thou of Israel? And I said unto her, Yea. And she said, And who is she that bringeth forth in the cave?

And I said, She that is bethrothed unto me. And she said to me, Is she not thy wife? And I said to her, It is Mary that was nurtured up in the temple of the Lord. And I received her to wife by lot, and she is not my wife, but she hath conception by the Holy Ghost. And the midwife said unto him, Is this the truth? And Joseph said unto her, Come hither and see.

And the midwife went with him. And they stood in the place of the cave. And beheld a bright cloud overshadowing the cave. And the midwife said, My soul is magnified this day, because mine eyes have seen marvellous things, for salvation is born unto Israel. And forthwith the cloud withdrew itself out of the cave, and a great light appeared in the cave so that our eyes could not endure it. And little by little that light withdrew itself until the young child appeared. And it went and took the breast of its mother Mary. And the midwife cried aloud and said, Great unto me today is this day, in that I have seen this new sight. And the midwife went forth of the cave and Salome met her. And she said to her, Salome, Salome, a new sight have I to tell thee. A virgin hath brought forth, which her nature alloweth not. And Salome said, As the Lord God liveth, if I make not trial and prove her nature I will not believe that a virgin hath brought forth.

And the midwife went in and said unto Mary, Order thyself, for there is no small contention arisen concerning thee. And Salome made trial and cried out and said, Woe unto mine iniquity and mine unbelief, because I have tempted the living God, and lo, my hand falleth away from me in fire. And she bowed her knees unto the Lord, saying, O God of my fathers, remember that I am the seed of Abraham and Isaac and Jacob, make me not a public example unto the children of Israel, but restore me unto the poor. For thou knowest, Lord, that in thy name did I perform my cures, and did receive my hire of thee.

And lo, an angel of the Lord appeared, saying unto her, Salome, Salome, the Lord hath hearkened to thee. Bring thine hand unto the young child and take him up, and there shall be unto thee salvation and joy.

BOOK OF JAMES OR PROTEVANGELIUM, 19.1–20.3.

Master of Flémalle, The Nativity, c 1420–30. Painting on wood.

Fine Arts Museum, Dijon.

When Joseph and Mary were on their way to Bethlehem, an Angel called a meeting of the Animals to see which ones should look after the Holy Family in the stable. The Lion stepped forward first. 'Only a king is worthy of serving the Lord of the World,' he roared. 'I will eat up anyone who comes too near the Child.'

'You are too frightening,' said the Angel.

Then the Fox slipped through to the front. 'I would serve them faithfully,' he simpered. 'I would find the sweetest honey for the Son of God, and every day I would steal a chicken for the Mother.'

'You are too sly,' said the Angel.

Many other animals came forward, but none of them had the right qualities. Finally, the Angel noticed the Ox and the Ass out in the fields, working for the farmer. The Angel called out to them, 'What can you offer us?' 'Nothing,' said the Ass, his ears flopping sadly down over his eyes. 'We have learned nothing except humility and patience. Anything else gets us a beating.' The Ox added, 'But perhaps we could drive off the flies with our tails, if that would be helpful.'

The Angel said, 'You are the ones I am looking for. Follow me.' And so the Ass and the Ox were led down to Bethlehem, and took their places in the stable.

'HOW THE ASS AND THE OX CAME TO THE CRIB', FOLK TALE.

Master of Hohenfurth, The Birth of Christ,

painting from the cycle Scenes from the Life of Christ, *c* 1350.

Tempera on wood. Narodny Gallery, Prague.

O Come, All ye Faithful

O come, all ye faithful, joyful and triumphant
O come ye, O come ye to Bethlehem;
Come and behold Him, born the king of angels;

Chorus
O come, let us adore Him,
O come, let us adore Him,
O come, let us adore Him,
Christ the Lord.

God from God, Light from Light eternal,
Lo! He abhors not the Virgin's womb;
Only begotten Son of the Father;

Chorus

Sing, choirs of angels, sing in exultation,
Sing, all ye citizens of heaven above;
Glory to God, glory in the highest;

Chorus

See how the shepherds, summoned to His cradle,
Leaving their flocks, draw nigh to gaze;
We too will thither bend our joyful footsteps;

Chorus

Child, for us sinners, poor and in the manger,
We would embrace thee, with love and awe;
Who would not love Thee, loving us so dearly?

Chorus

Lo! star-led chieftains, magi, Christ adoring,
Offer Him frankincense and gold and myrrh;
We to the Christ-child bring our hearts' oblations;

Chorus

JOHN FRANCIS WADE, 'O COME,
ALL YE FAITHFUL', c 1743.

Master of Paciano, The Adoration of the Magi, 1315–50.
Painting on wood. National Gallery of Umbria, Perugia.

Long, Long Ago

Winds thro' the olive trees
    Softly did blow,
Round little Bethlehem
    Long, long ago.

Sheep on the hillside lay
    Whiter than snow;
Shepherds were watching them,
    Long, long ago.

Then from the happy sky,
    Angels bent low,
Singing their songs of joy,
    Long, long ago.

For in a manger bed,
    Cradled we know,
Christ came to Bethlehem,
    Long, long ago.

ANON, CHRISTMAS POEM.

Book of Hours for use in Paris, Nativity, folio 48.

Illuminated manuscript on parchment. Museum of the Middle Ages, Cluny.

*W*EIGH NOT HIS CRIB, HIS WOODEN DISH,

NOR BEASTS THAT ROUND HIM PRESS;

WEIGH NOT HIS MOTHER'S POOR ATTIRE

NOR JOSEPH'S SIMPLE DRESS.

THE STABLE IS A PRINCE'S COURT,

THE CRIB HIS CHAIR OF STATE;

THE BEASTS ARE PARCEL OF HIS POMP,

THE WOODEN DISH HIS PLATE.

ROBERT SOUTHWELL, c 1561–1595, 'NEW PRINCE, NEW POMP'.

Fragment of a Nativity, *Brussels, end 15th century. Relief in walnut. Louvre Museum, Paris.*

Italian School, The Nativity, *15th century.*

Miniature on vellum. Musée Bonnat, Bayonne.

No touch of winter's frosty breath,

No snowclad fields 'neath skies that lower;

All Nature thrills with joyous life,

As faintly from the distant tower

Ring out the cheerful Christmas Bells.

Hark! how their cadence softly swells

O'er open fields and bosky dells,

'In Excelsis Gloria!'

'Neath skies of blue the plains lie decked

In thousand varying shades of green.

Soft shadows sweep o'er meadows gay

With many a floweret's brilliant sheen;

While Christmas Bells in glad refrain

Sound the glad tidings once again

Which angels sang in raptured strain,

'In Excelsis Gloria!'

NEW ZEALAND CAROL.

Hark! the Herald Angels Sing

Hark! the herald angels sing
Glory to the newborn King!
Peace on earth and mercy mild.
God and sinners reconciled!
Joyful, all ye nations, rise,
Join the triumph of the skies;
With the angelic host proclaim
Christ is born in Bethlehem!

Chorus
Hark! the herald angels sing
Glory to the newborn King!

Christ, by highest heaven adored;
Christ, the everlasting Lord;
Late in time behold Him come,
Offspring of a Virgin's womb,
Veiled in flesh the Godhead see;
Hail the incarnate Deity.
Pleased as man with man to dwell;
Jesus, our Emmanuel!

Chorus

Mild he lays His glory by,
Born that we no more may die,
Born to raise us from the earth,
Born to give us second birth.
Risen with healing in His wings,
Light and life to all He brings,
Hail, the Sun of Righteousness!
Hail, the heaven-born Prince of
Peace!

Chorus

CHARLES WESLEY, 'HARK! THE
HERALD ANGELS SING', 1739.

Master of Raigern,
The Birth of Christ, *c* 1425.
Painted panel from a retable in pinewood.
Kunsthistorischesmuseum, Vienna.

Giotto di Bondone, The Presentation of
Jesus at the Temple, *detail*, 1303–5.
Fresco. Scrovegni Chapel, Padua.

What Can I Give Him?

What can I give Him,
Poor as I am?
If I were a shepherd
I would bring a lamb,
If I were a wise man
I would do my part
Yet what I can I give Him
– Give my heart.

CHRISTINA ROSSETTI, 1830–1894,
'A CHRISTMAS CAROL'.

Giotto di Bondone, The Nativity, *detail*, 1303–5.
Fresco. Scrovegni Chapel, Padua.

Andrea della Robbia, Adoration of the Magi, 1435–1525.

Glazed terracotta. Victoria and Albert Museum, London.

Once in Royal David's City

Once in royal David's city
Stood a lowly cattle shed,
Where a mother laid her baby
In a manger for His bed:
Mary was that mother mild,
Jesus Christ her little child.

He came down to earth from heaven,
Who is God and Lord of all,
And His shelter was a stable,
And His cradle was a stall:
With the poor, the meek and lowly,
Lived on earth our Saviour holy.

And our eyes at last shall see Him,
Through His own redeeming love:
For that Child who seemed so helpless
Is our Lord in heaven above:
And He leads His children on
To the place where He is gone.

Not in that poor lowly stable,
With the oxen standing by,
We shall see Him, but in heaven,
Set at God's right hand on high:
When like stars His children crowned,
All in white shall wait around.

CECIL FRANCIS ALEXANDER,
'ONCE IN ROYAL DAVID'S CITY', 1848.

W rapped in His swaddling bands,
And in His manger laid,
The Hope and Glory of all lands
Is come to the world's aid:
No peaceful home upon His cradle smiled,
Guests rudely came and went, where slept the royal Child.

But where Thou dwellest, Lord,
No other thought should be,
Once duly welcomed and adored,
How should I part with Thee?
Bethlehem must lose Thee soon, but Thou wilt grace
The single heart to be Thy sure abiding-place.

Thee, on the bosom laid
Of a pure virgin mind,
In quiet ever, and in shade,
Shepherd and sage may find;
They, who have bowed untaught to Nature's sway,
And they, who follow Truth along her star-paved way.

The pastoral spirits first
Approach Thee, Babe divine,
For they in lowly thoughts are nursed,
Meet for Thy lowly shrine:
Sooner than they should miss where Thou dost dwell,
Angels from Heaven will stoop to guide them to Thy cell.

JOHN KEBLE, 'CHRISTMAS DAY'
FROM THE CHRISTIAN YEAR, 1827.

François Boucher, The Light of the World, 1750.

Oil on wood. Fine Arts Museum, Lyon.

At the time of the Lord's birth, three Magi came to Jerusalem. Their Latin names were Appelius, Amerius and Damascus; in Hebrew they were called Galgalat, Malgalat and Sarathin; in Greek they were Caspar, Balthasar and Melchior. But who were these Magi? There are three ways of looking at this, for the word Magi has three meanings. Magi can be deceivers, magicians or wise men. Some claim that the three kings were called Magi, or deceivers, because they deceived Herod by not returning to him. The Gospel says of Herod: 'when he saw that he was mocked of the wise men'.

Magus, in the singular, can also mean magician. Pharaoh's magicians were called Magi, and St Chrysostom says that this is where their name comes from. According to him, they were magicians who had been converted. The Lord wished to reveal His birth to them, and so he drew them to Him and in this way gave sinners the hope that they too might be pardoned. Magus is also the word for a wise man. For Magus in Hebrew means scribe, in Greek philosopher, in Latin wise man. So they were called Magi, that is to say learned men, or marvellously wise beings.

JACOBUS DE VORAGINE, THE GOLDEN LEGEND, 1261–66.

Pierre Spicre, The Three Magi, *Tapestry of the Life of the Virgin Mary*, 1474–1500. Notre-Dame Collegiate Church, Beaune.

Pieter Brueghel the Younger, The Adoration of the Magi, 1564–1638.

Oil on wood. Hermitage Museum, St Petersburg.

WE THREE KINGS OF ORIENT ARE

WE THREE KINGS OF ORIENT ARE,
BEARING GIFTS WE TRAVERSE AFAR,
FIELD AND FOUNTAIN,
MOOR AND MOUNTAIN,
FOLLOWING YONDER STAR.

CHORUS
O STAR OF WONDER, STAR OF NIGHT,
STAR WITH ROYAL BEAUTY BRIGHT;
WESTWARD LEADING, STILL PROCEEDING,
GUIDE US TO THY PERFECT LIGHT!

BORN A KING ON BETHLEHEM'S PLAIN,
GOLD I BRING TO CROWN HIM AGAIN,
KING FOR EVER,
CEASING NEVER
OVER US ALL TO REIGN.

CHORUS

FRANKINCENSE TO OFFER HAVE I
INCENSE OWNS A DEITY NIGH;
PRAYER AND PRAISING,
GLADLY RAISING,
WORSHIP HIM, GOD MOST HIGH.

CHORUS

MYRHH IS MINE; ITS BITTER PERFUME
BREATHES A LIFE OF GATHERING GLOOM;
SORROWING, SIGHING,
BLEEDING, DYING,
SEALED IN THE STONE-COLD TOMB.

CHORUS

GLORIOUS NOW BEHOLD HIM ARISE,
KING AND GOD AND SACRIFICE;
HEAVEN SINGS
ALLELUIA, ALLELUIA
THE EARTH REPLIES.

CHORUS

JOHN HENRY HOPKINS, JR, 'WE THREE KINGS OF ORIENT ARE', 1857.

Gentile da Fabriano, Adoration of the Magi, 1423. Tempera on wood. Uffizi Gallery, Florence.

The Adoration of the Magi, *Germany, 15th century. Illumination.*
National Library of Austria, Vienna.

What gift shall we bring to Thee,

O Christ, since Thou as Man on earth

For us hast shewn Thyself?

Since every creature made by Thee

Brings to Thee its thanksgiving.

The angels bring their song,

The heavens bring their star,

The Magi bring their gifts,

The shepherds bring their awe,

Earth gives a cave,

The wilderness a manger,

And we the Virgin-Mother bring.

God before all worlds, have mercy upon us!

HYMN OF ST ANATOLIUS, 5TH CENTURY.

Herod

OH, GOOD WISE MEN,
COME IN AND DINE;
I WILL GIVE YOU
BOTH BEER AND WINE,
AND HAY AND STRAW
TO MAKE YOUR BED,
AND NOUGHT OF PAYMENT
SHALL BE SAID.

The Wise Men

OH, NO! OH, NO!
WE MUST AWAY,
WE SEEK A LITTLE
CHILD TODAY,
A LITTLE CHILD,
A MIGHTY KING,
HIM WHO CREATED
EVERYTHING.

FROM A MEDIEVAL CAROL.

Jacquelin de Montluçon,
The Adoration of the Child, 15th century.
Oil on wood. Fine Arts Museum, Dijon.

While Shepherds Watched

While shepherds watch'd their flocks by night,
All seated on the ground,
The Angel of the Lord came down,
And glory shone around.

Fear not, said he, for mighty dread
Had seized their troubled minds;
Glad tidings of great joy I bring
To you and all mankind.

To you in David's town, this day
Is born of David's line
A Saviour who is Christ the Lord;
And this shall be the sign.

The heavenly Babe ye there shall find
To human view display'd,
All meanly wrapp'd in swaddling bands,
And in a manger laid.

Thus spake the seraph, and forthwith
Appeared a shining throng
Of angels praising God, who thus
Addressed their joyful song.

All glory be to God on high
And on earth be peace;
Goodwill henceforth from heaven to men
Begin and never cease.

NAHUM TATE, 'WHILE SHEPHERDS WATCHED', 1700.

Book of Hours, The Annunciation to the Shepherds, MS 6, *folio* 41,
France, *c* 1480. Miniature. Pierpont Morgan Library, New York.

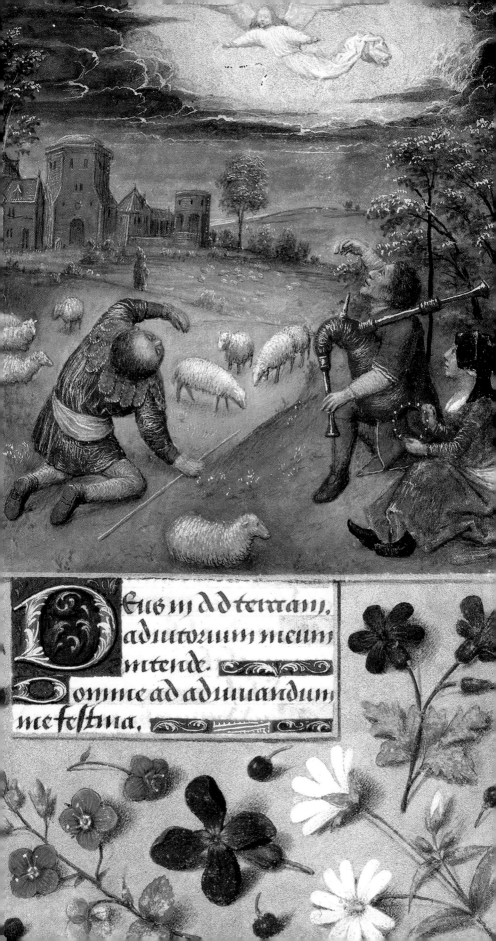

Deus in adiutorium meum intende. Domine ad adiuvandum me festina.

THE TWELVE DAYS
OF CHRISTMAS

CHRISTMAS EVE TO EPIPHANY

he festival of Christmas extends from
Christmas Eve on 24 December to the
Feast of the Epiphany on 6 January.
Although it has long been commonly accepted that
Jesus was born on 25 December, Epiphany festivals vary
according to where they take place. Broadly, this is the
day the Western Church celebrates the journey of the
Magi to see the Infant Jesus, while the Eastern Church
commemorates the baptism of Jesus.

Falling as it does in the middle of winter in the Northern
Hemisphere, the cycle of feasts celebrated in Europe at
Christmas coincides and overlaps with other, more ancient
beliefs and customs from pagan and pre-Christian times.
Above all, the Twelve Days were filled with superstitions
and 'bewitchments', supernatural companions to the
darkness naturally prevailing at that time of year, along
with howling winds and stormy heaths and hillsides
patrolled by ghosts, witches and other mischief-makers.
People were led astray by Will o' the Wisp, or followed by
black dogs, werewolves, vampires and hideous monsters

Previous page:
Neapolitan crib, 18th
century. Musée de
Chaumont, France.

Three Angels
Singing the Gloria,
end 15th century.
Wall ornament.
Polychromy and
gilding on limestone.
Burgundy, France.

from the underworld. It was not a time to go out after dark, farmers locked up their sheep and cattle in case evil fairies got amongst them, and some jobs were banned for the Twelve Days, such as threshing and spinning flax. Belief in similar spirits can be found all over the world, and in New Zealand, for example, a stronghold of shepherds and sheep-farming, the spirit legends of Maori culture have been absorbed into the Christmas story.

★ ★★

The Nativity,
12th century.
Byzantine mosaic.
Church of the
Martorana, Palermo.

The great event of this whole period is, of course, the Birth of Christ on 25 December, which was first celebrated in Rome around the middle of the 4th century. Gradually, the festival spread through the West. St Augustine brought

it with him from Rome, and on Christmas Day 598, more than 10,000 English converts were baptised. In the Middle Ages, Christmas became an increasingly warm and merry occasion. People experienced great joy in the story of Jesus, who was seen as a real child to be cosseted and rocked in the manger. This was the Christmas of Noëls and carol-singing, lullabies and hymns – songs to celebrate the wonder of the Incarnation, the 'Gloria in Excelsis'.

★ ★★

In south-eastern Europe, Jesus was traditionally born in a cave or grotto, and this motif is faithfully repeated in icons of the Nativity from Cyprus to Russia. Some of these portray group scenes with Magi, shepherds, angels, farm animals and midwives giving the new-born Christ a ritual bath. In other icons, the Mother appears alone, holding the Child in her arms.

In Italy, and westwards into France, Spain and Portugal, it is the crib – the 'living crèche' – that forms the focus of attention. These range from simple stable scenes, set up in a

Mother and Child, *19th century.* *Icon from Cyprus.* *Private collection.*

corner of the church, in the village square or in private homes, to much more elaborate stagings – perhaps a fully lit model village, representing Bethlehem. St Francis is widely credited with founding this tradition, when he ordered a crib to be set up in the Italian town of Grecchio. Over the centuries, the designing of Christmas cribs became a specialist craft. In Provence, they developed a special cast of miniature figures, 'little saints', to decorate the scene. The craftsmen of Naples were especially skilful and imaginative, and even today the city's churches vie with each other to produce the most beautiful crèche of the year – to the great delight of their parishioners. In Alaska, by contrast, the Coming of Jesus is announced by taking a star on a pole from door to door; the main procession is followed by a group of Herod's Men, who try to capture the star. Various folk customs are linked to the three saints' days that follow Christmas – St Stephen's (26 December), St John the Evangelist's (27 December) and the Holy Innocents' (28 December). St Stephen is the patron saint of horses, and in Europe his day is a great occasion for horse races and expeditions on horseback. In Sweden, horses were ridden to drink from water that flowed northwards; this was the 'cream of the water' and would keep them healthy in the coming year.

Neapolitan crib, 17th century. Mahogany, ebony and ivory. Musée Bonaparte, Ajaccio.

★ ★ ★

On St John's Day, wine was taken to church in various parts of Germany to be blessed by the priest and then taken home to be drunk there. This wine was meant to protect people drinking it from being struck by lightning, and in Bavaria it was used as medicine.

Many superstitions are attached to Holy Inocents' Day, or Childermas, because of the Massacre of the Innocents by Herod. It was said to be an unlucky day, particularly for doing any work, and Edward IV of England is said to have postponed his coronation because it was originally arranged for Childermas.

The dominant features of New Year's Eve and New Year's Day are the exchange of good wishes and charms, and ceremonies to create good omens for the future.

In 19th-century New York, people visited their neighbours and friends in a day-long party of noisy and hilarious greetings, drinking a glass of wine and dashing away to the next house. This custom relates to the many 'first-footing' rituals which flourish from Scotland to Macedonia. The first person to cross the threshold on New Year's Day usually brings a lucky gift – a piece of coal, whisky or a sprig of evergreens. Elsewhere, the visitor walks straight to the hearth and strikes new sparks from the Christmas log. Meanwhile, the search for good omens about the coming year is a universal need. In some Greek islands, the head of the family picks up a stone on the way back from church, and all the family pray that in the New Year they will receive 'as much gold as the weight of the stone'.

At Epiphany, the Feast of the Three Kings is celebrated in Spain and Italy with presents for children. In Italy the Befana, a kindly old woman, brings presents round in a sack, while in Spain the Three Kings are said to be travelling to Bethlehem to adore the Infant Jesus. On their way, they call with

In Italy, the Befana brings presents at Epiphany. Illustration, 1867. Kharbine-Tapabor collection, Paris.

presents for the children, who put out shoes on their window ledges or balconies, together with straw for the Kings' horses.

In older ceremonies, notably in England, France, Holland and Germany, family and other groups elected a 'king' for the day, perhaps a descendant of the ancient king of the Saturnalia, the lord of the revels in Imperial Rome. A festive cake known as the Twelfth Cake was shared by all present. Sometimes an extra slice was held back for the next visitor; by custom this was the leader of a band of children, who rewarded his hosts by singing a song. In other areas, the first two slices were reserved for God and the Blessed Virgin, and given to the first poor person to present himself.

A Virgin Most Pure

A virgin most pure,
As the prophets foretold,
Should bring forth a Saviour
Which we now behold,
To be our Redeemer
From death, hell and sin,
Which Adam's transgression
Involved us in.

Chorus:
Then therefore be merry,
Cast sorrows aside;
Christ Jesus our Saviour
Was born on this tide.

TRADITIONAL CHRISTMAS SONG.

'Whom saw ye O shepherds? speak;
tell us who hath appeared on the earth.'

'We saw the new-born Child, and angels
singing praise unto the Lord.'

'Speak, what saw ye? and tell us of the
birth of Christ.'

'We saw the new-born Child, and angels
singing praise unto the Lord.'

RESPONSORY FOR CHRISTMAS MATINS.

Domenikos Theotocopoulos, known as El Greco,
Adoration of the Shepherds, 1540–1614.
Prado Museum, Madrid.

Away in a Manger

Away in a manger,
No crib for a bed,
The little Lord Jesus
Laid down His sweet head,
The stars in the bright sky
Looked down where He lay,
The little Lord Jesus
Asleep on the hay.

The cattle are lowing,
The Baby awakes,
But little Lord Jesus
No crying He makes,
I love Thee, Lord Jesus,
Look down from the sky,
And stay by my side
Til morning is nigh.

Be near me, Lord Jesus,
I ask Thee to stay
Close by me forever,
And love me, I pray.
Bless all the dear children
In Thy tender care,
And fit us for heaven
To live with Thee there.

TRADITIONAL CAROL.

Catalan School, The Nativity, 12th century. Oil on wood. Church of Sagos. Diocesan Museum, Solsona.

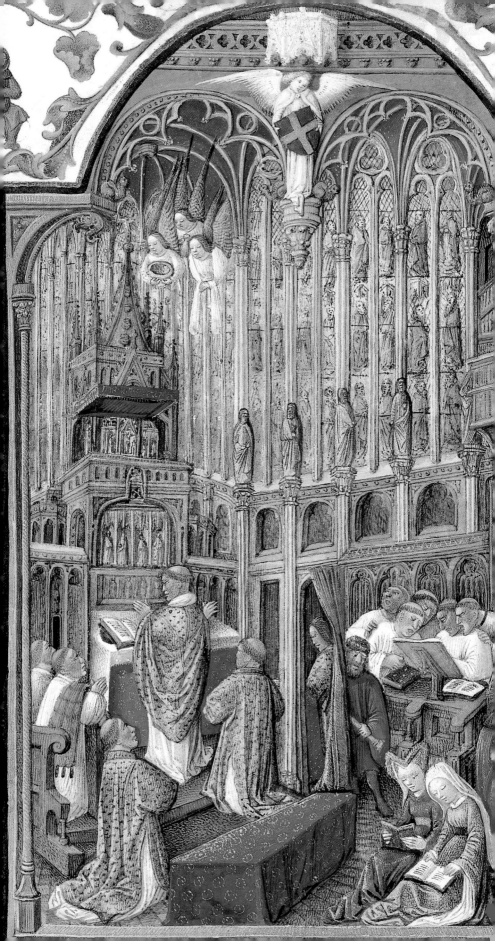

I can see myself as a little girl,

bundled up to the tip of my nose in furs and knitted shawls, tiny wooden shoes on my feet, a lantern in my hand, setting out for the Midnight Mass of Christmas Eve .... We started off, a number of us, together in a stream of light .... Our lanterns cast great shadows on the white road, crisp with frost. As our little group advanced it saw others on their way, people from the farm and from the mill, who joined us, and once on the Place de l'Eglise we found ourselves with all the parishioners in a body. No-one spoke – the icy north wind cut short our breath; but the voice of the chimes filled the silence .... We entered, accompanied by a gust of wind that swept into the porch at the same time as we did; and the splendours of the altar, studded with lights, green with pine and laurel branches, dazzled us from the threshold.

MME TH BENTZON, 'CHRISTMAS IN FRANCE' IN THE
CENTURY MAGAZINE, NEW YORK, 1901.

Les Très Riches Heures du duc de Berry, The Christmas Mass, 15th century.
Illuminated manuscript. Musée Condé, Chantilly.

In the Holy Nativity
of our Lord

Gloomy night embrac'd the place
Where the Noble Infant lay;
The Babe look'd up and show'd his face,
In spite of darkness, it was day.
It was thy day, Sweet! and did rise
Not from the east, but from thine eyes.
Chorus
It was thy day, Sweet! and did rise
Not from the east, but from thine eyes.

We saw thee in thy balmy nest,
Young dawn of our eternal day!
We saw thine eyes break from their east
And chase the trembling shades away.
We saw thee, and we blessed the sight,
We saw thee by thine own sweet light.
Chorus
We saw thee, and we blessed the sight,
We saw thee by thine own sweet light.

Poor World, said I, what wilt thou do
To entertain this starry stranger?
Is this the best thou canst bestow,
A cold, and not too cleanly, manger?
Contend, ye powers of heav'n and earth,
To fit a bed for this huge birth.
Chorus
Contend, ye powers of heav'n and earth,
To fit a bed for this huge birth.

RICHARD CRASHAW,
'IN THE HOLY NATIVITY OF OUR LORD', 1646.

Crib in wax, end 18th century. Musée des Arts et Traditions Populaires, Paris.

*T*HITHER COME THE PEOPLE, BEARING HUMBLE GIFTS OF CHESTNUTS, APPLES, TOMATOES AND THE LIKE, WHICH THEY PLACE AS OFFERINGS IN THE HANDS OF THE FIGURES. THESE ARE VERY OFTEN LIFE-SIZE. MARY IS USUALLY ROBED IN BLUE SATIN, WITH CRIMSON SCARF AND WHITE HEADDRESS. JOSEPH STANDS NEAR HER DRESSED IN THE ORDINARY WORKING GARB. THE ONLOOKERS ARE GOT UP LIKE ITALIAN CONTADINI. THE MAGI ARE ALWAYS VERY PROMINENT IN THEIR GRAND CLOTHES, WITH SATIN TRAINS BORNE BY BLACK SLAVES, JEWELLED TURBANS, AND SATIN TUNICS ALL OVER JEWELS.

W H D ROUSE, 'RELIGIOUS TABLEAUX
IN ITALIAN CHURCHES', 1894.

Neapolitan crib, 18th century.

Royal Palace, Caserta, Italy.

Crib, The Journey of the Three Magi from the East. *20th century.*

Epiphany Play

... ON THE DAY OF THE EPIPHANY, THREE CLERICS, ROBED AS KINGS, SHALL COME FROM THE EAST, NORTH AND SOUTH, AND MEET BEFORE THE ALTAR, WITH THEIR SERVANTS BEARING THE OFFERINGS OF THE MAGI. THE KING FROM THE EAST, POINTING TO THE STAR WITH HIS STICK, EXCLAIMS:

'THE STAR GLOWS WITH EXCEEDING BRIGHTNESS.'

THE SECOND MONARCH ANSWERS: 'WHICH SHOWS THE BIRTH OF THE KING OF KINGS.'

AND THE THIRD: 'TO WHOSE COMING THE PROPHECIES OF OLD HAD POINTED.'

THEN THE MAGI KISS ONE ANOTHER AND TOGETHER SING: 'LET US THEREFORE GO AND SEEK HIM, OFFERING UNTO HIM GIFTS: GOLD, FRANKINCENSE AND MYRRH.'

... THE MAGI GO TO AN ALTAR ABOVE WHICH AN IMAGE OF THE VIRGIN HAS BEEN PLACED WITH A LIGHTED STAR BEFORE IT. TWO PRIESTS ... BID THEM APPROACH TO WORSHIP THE CHILD, 'FOR HE IS THE REDEMPTION OF THE WORLD'. THE THREE KINGS DO ADORATION, AND OFFER THEIR GIFTS:

'RECEIVE, O KING, GOLD.'

'ACCEPT INCENSE, THOU VERY GOD.'

'MYRRH, THE SIGN OF BURIAL.'

EPIPHANY PLAY FROM ROUEN, FRANCE.

The Manger

When I was present by the manger of the Lord in Bethlehem, I beheld a virgin of extreme beauty well wrapped in a white mantle and a delicate tunic through which I clearly perceived her virgin body. With her was an old man of great honesty, and they brought with them an ox and an ass. These entered the cave, and the man tied them to the manger, then went outside and brought the Virgin a burning candle, and having attached this to the wall, he went outside again so that he might not be present at the birth. Then the Virgin pulled off the shoes from her feet, drew off the white mantle that enveloped her, removed the veil from her head, laying it by her side, thus remaining in her tunic alone, with her beautiful golden hair falling loosely over her shoulders. Then she produced two small linen cloths and two woollen ones of exquisite purity and fineness which she had brought to wrap up the Child who was to be born.

ST BRIDGET, REVELATIONS, PUBLISHED 1492.
ST BRIDGET (C 1303–73) MADE HER JOURNEY
TO THE HOLY LAND IN 1372.

Figures in spun glass from Nevers, end 18th century.

Musée du Vieux-Marseille, Marseilles.

St Francis and the Crib

About fifteen days before the birthday of Christ, Francis summoned John and said to him, 'If you wish to celebrate the Feast of the Lord at Greccio, go with haste and diligently prepare what I tell you. I want to do something to recall the memory of that Child who was born in Bethlehem, to see with bodily eyes the inconveniences of his infancy, how He lay in the manger, and how the ox and the ass stood by.' Upon hearing this, the good and faithful man went off to prepare all that the holy man had requested.

The day of joy drew near. With glad hearts, the men and women of that place prepared, according to their means, candles and torches to light up that night which has illuminated all the days and years with its glittering star.

At length, the manger was ready, the hay brought, the ox and ass were led in. Simplicity was honoured there, poverty exalted, humility was commended and a new Bethlehem was made from Greccio. The night was lighted up like the day, delighting men and beasts. The people came and joyfully celebrated the new mystery. The woods rang with voices and the rocks responded to their rejoicing. The brothers sang, discharging their debt of praise to the Lord, and the whole night echoed with jubilation.

The saint of God stood before the manger full of sighs, consumed by devotion and filled with a wonderful happiness. The solemnities of the mass were performed over the manger and the priest knew a new consolation.

THOMAS OF CELANO, 'ST FRANCIS AND THE CRIB', c 1248.

Detail of a Neopolitan crib, 18th century, Musée de Chaumont, France.

St Nicholas, Santa Claus and Father Christmas

T he original St Nicholas has become two people. Until the 19th century, it was all much easier. St Nicholas was the 4th-century bishop of Myra in ancient Lycia, now Demre in Turkey. He performed many miracles, and became the patron saint of boys and mariners. The story of one miracle tells how he restored three boys to life 7 years after a wicked butcher had killed them, cut them up and hidden them in his brine tub. The saint's feast, on 6 December, probably started as a beginning-of-winter festival, and shares many features with that of St Martin on 11 November. Both saints brought sweet things for the good children and punishment rods for the bad. The figure of St Nicholas was mimed by a local man dressed as a bishop, with mitre and pastoral staff, and attended by a grotesque figure sometimes known as Krampus. As the saint made his rounds, children who knew their catechism were rewarded with nuts, gingerbread or toys from his basket. If they did not, St Nicholas called the fearsome Krampus into action.

Opposite: Alexandre Hesse, Saint Nicholas, 19th century. Mural painting. Church of Chevry-en-Sereine.

Krampus, the German monster, end 19th century. Kharbine-Tapabor collection, Paris.

91

The real St Nicholas is buried at the seaport of Bari in Italy. His tomb is a place of pilgrimage, and on 8 May each year, in a spectacular show of faith, sailors of the port take the saint's image out to sea. At nightfall they return with it and form a magnificent torchlit procession back to the cathedral, singing chants while fireworks explode all around them.

★ ★★

In the Dutch tradition, Sinter Claes also arrived in Amsterdam by water, where he was welcomed by the local dignitaries and then set off to visit all the children, accompanied by his mischievous attendant Black Piet. Again, good children were

Jost Amman, Saint Nicholas riding an Ass, dressed as 'Vielfrass' the Glutton, 1539–91. Pen drawing heightened with white. Louvre Museum, Paris.

rewarded and bad children received nothing. Later, Sinter Claes was taken by Dutch settlers to New Amsterdam, now New York, where he was established under the Dutch dialect name of Sinte Klaas. Once this name had been anglicised as Santa Claus, a worldwide figure and children's favourite came into being whose fame and jolly features have spread as far as China, Japan and Africa, where in non-Christian areas he is celebrated as a bringer of good luck for the coming year.

★ ★★

Germany is an important source for many things associated with Christmas, influential also through its many settlers in the United States and elsewhere. In Germany itself, St Nicholas acquired a rival in the early 17th century, when a Protestant pastor began urging parents not to tell their children that it was St Nicholas who brought their presents but the Christ Child (*das Christkind*), for 'the holy Christ Child gives us all the good things for body and soul, and it is He alone we should call upon'. From those beginnings, the Christ Child became a kind of mythical figure, a tall child with long fair hair, often represented by a girl dressed in white. He is not so much an updated image of

the Holy Infant as a kind of angel or good fairy, whose role is to bring presents for children, surrounded by picturesque attendants.

As for the presents themselves, the steady commercialisation of Christmas since the Second World War, along with the rising expectations of people in the developed countries, has seen to it that much of the old simplicity has been lost. On the other hand, Christmas is also a time of giving to the poor and needy, and the number of money-raising campaigns and charity sales at this time of year testify to a widespread sense of solidarity and mutual aid. Perhaps,

Left: Didoukh, a 'Christmas tree' made from ears of oats, Western Ukraine. Private collection.

Christmas Market, 1891. *Lithograph from a painting by Ludwig Blume-Siebert. Archiv für Kunst und Geschichte, Berlin.*

though, we sometimes lose sight of the idea that presents need only be tokens, small gifts to be exchanged between those closest to us, and that not so very long ago a Christmas sock or stocking was not expected to hold more than a few nuts and apples (the most traditional gifts), some sugar-plums or a cake, and a simple toy.

★ ★ ★

The sight of a Christmas tree lifts people's hearts like no other seasonal plant. It is most strongly associated with the dense forests of Middle Europe, where it lives in such abundance. Some say that it was Martin Luther who started the Christmas tree tradition when he set up for his children a tree lit by dozens of candles, a vision of the starry heavens from which Christ came down to Earth. By the 18th century, Christmas trees were becoming more common, at first among landed and well-to-do urban families, then over the years the fashion spread. By 1890, the shops and markets in Paris were selling upwards of 30,000 trees each year. Today, the Christmas markets of Europe, notably those in Nuremberg, Salzburg and Strasbourg, are the targets for tourists from all over the world, each a dazzling spectacle of brilliant lights and candles, and rows of stalls selling everything from Christmas trees and decorations to glittering craft jewellery, cakes and spiced loaves, novelty presents, and sizzling sausages and Glühwein to restore the weary shopper. In the islands of Hawaii, they have more nautical traditions. Santa Claus arrives by boat, and the Christmas season begins with the coming of the Christmas Tree Ship, with its cargo of traditional Christmas fare.

Picking Holly, book illustration for A Letter to Santa Claus, *Ed Berger Publ. Company, New York,* 1907.

The practice of decorating the house with evergreens has been with us since the Roman Empire. Everywhere that Christmas falls in winter, plants such as holly, ivy and mistletoe, which bear fruit at this time, are prized not only for their freshness and colour, but also because they symbolise the unending cycle of life within the plant world. In the Southern Hemisphere, where Christmas falls in high summer, other plants have taken over this role. In Australia, where Santa Claus sweeps into the seaside beaches on water-skis, the best-known seasonal trees and plants are the Christmas Bush, a red-leaved tree, Christmas Bells with their long drooping dark-red bell-flowers, and the yellow-flowering Western Australia Christmas tree. Families also decorate their homes with a branch from a pine tree or a eucalyptus.

★ ★ ★

Another age-old and charming tradition is the lighting of the Yule log, placed on the fire for the Vigil of the Nativity. The log itself not only gave out gratifying warmth, it was also seen as possessing special properties, its glow securing the vital services of the sun in the coming year, and asserting the values of the sacred hearth-fire, the centre of all family life. The ceremonial aspect was especially strong in southern Slav countries, and also in the South of France, where the whole family went out to bring in the log, which was usually cut from a fruit tree. It was carried home with the oldest member of the family at one end and the youngest at the other. In some places they toured the kitchen with it three times, and wine was poured on it in the name of the Father, Son and Holy Ghost. Then the log was laid on the fire, and all the candles in the room were lit. After Christmas, the charcoal was kept all the coming year to protect the family. Placed under the bed, it guarded them against lightning. People touched it to ensure they would not get chilblains, and in the stables it protected animals against various diseases. Ashes from the log were placed in wells to keep the water pure.

Thomas Nast,
A Boy Hangs Up
His Stocking for
Presents.
Drawing for Harper's
Weekly, 1876.

ON A DAY, AS A SHIP WITH MARINERS WERE
IN PERISHING ON THE SEA, THEY PRAYED AND REQUIRED DEVOUTLY
NICHOLAS, SERVANT OF GOD, SAYING: IF THOSE THINGS THAT
WE HAVE HEARD OF THEE SAID BE TRUE, PROVE THEM NOW.
AND ANON A MAN APPEARED IN HIS LIKENESS, AND SAID: LO!
SEE YE ME NOT? YE CALLED ME, AND THEN HE BEGAN TO HELP
THEM IN THEIR EXPLOIT OF THE SEA, AND ANON THE TEMPEST
CEASED. AND WHEN THEY WERE COME TO HIS CHURCH, THEY
KNEW HIM WITHOUT ANY MAN TO SHOW HIM TO THEM, AND YET
THEY HAD NEVER SEEN HIM. AND THEN THEY THANKED GOD AND HIM
OF THEIR DELIVERANCE. AND HE BADE THEM TO ATTRIBUTE IT TO THE
MERCY OF GOD, AND TO THEIR BELIEF, AND NOTHING TO HIS MERITS.

JACOBUS DE VORAGINE, THE GOLDEN LEGEND, 1275.
'ENGLISHED' BY WILLIAM CAXTON, 1483.

Saint Nicholas, patron saint of sailors, miraculously calming the storm, according to Eastern tradition, 17th century. Fresco from a church at Delphi.

Saint Nicholas and Eighteen Scenes Showing His
Life and Miracles, *Russian icon, 15th–16th century.*
Tempera on wood. Russian National Museum, St Petersburg.

In the far-off Polar seas,
Far beyond the Hebrides,
Where the icebergs, towering high,
Seem to pierce the wintry sky,
And the fur-clad Esquimaux
Glide in sledges o'er the snow,
Dwells St Nick, the merry wight,
Patron saint of Christmas night.

Solid walls of massive ice,
Bearing many a quaint device,
Flanked by graceful turrets twain,
Clear as clearest porcelain,
Bearing at a lofty height
Christ's pure cross in simple white,
Carven with surpassing art
From an iceberg's crystal heart.

Here St Nick, in royal state,
Dwells, until December late
Clips the days at either end,
And the nights at each extend;
Then with his attendant sprites,
Scours the earth on wintry nights,
Bringing home in well-filled hands,
Children's gifts from many lands.

Here are whistles, tops and toys,
Meant to gladden little boys;
Skates and sleds that soon will glide
O'er the ice or steep hill-side.
Here are dolls with flaxen curls,
Sure to charm the little girls;
Christmas books, with pictures gay,
For this welcome holiday.

HORATIO ALGER, 'ST NICHOLAS', 1832–99.

Saint Nicholas, *coloured print from the Vosges, printed by Pelerin.*

Musée des Arts et Traditions Populaires, Paris.

'Twas the night before Christmas

'Twas the night before Christmas, when all through the house

Not a creature was stirring, not even a mouse;

The stockings were hung by the chimney with care,

In hopes that St Nicholas soon would be there;

The children were nestled all snug in their beds,

While visions of sugar-plums danced in their heads;

And mamma in her 'kerchief, and I in my cap,

Had just settled down for a long winter's nap,

When out on the lawn there arose such a clatter,

I sprang from the bed to see what was the matter.

Away to the window I flew like a flash,

Tore open the shutters and threw up the sash.

The moon on the breast of the new-fallen snow

Gave the lustre of mid-day to objects below,

When, what to my wondering eyes should appea

But a miniature sleigh, and eight tiny reindeer

With a little old driver, so lively and quick,

I knew in a moment it must be St Nick.

More rapid than eagles his coursers they came,

And he whistled, and shouted, and called them by nan

Saint Nicholas,
early 20th century.
Chromolithograph.

Father Christmas Brings Presents, end 19th century. Chromolithograph. Kharbine-Tapabor collection Paris.

Now, Dasher! now, Dancer! Now, Prancer and Vixen!

On, Comet! On, Cupid! On, Donner and Blitzen!

To the top of the porch! to the top of the wall!

Now dash away! dash away! dash away all!

As dry leaves that before the wild hurricane fly,

When they meet with an obstacle, mount to the sky,

So up to the house-top the coursers they flew,

With the sleigh full of toys, and St Nicholas too.

And then, in a twinkling, I heard on the roof,

The prancing and pawing of each little hoof.

As I drew in my hand, and was turning around,

Down the chimney St Nicholas came with a bound.

He was dressed all in fur,

from his head to his foot,

And his clothes were all tarnished

with ashes and soot;

A bundle of toys he had flung

on his back,

And he looked like a peddler just

opening his pack.

His eyes – how they twinkled!

His dimples how merry!

His cheeks were like roses,

his nose like a cherry!

His droll little mouth was drawn

up like a bow,

And the beard of his chin was as

white as the snow;

The stump of a pipe he held

tight in his teeth,

And the smoke it encircled his

head like a wreath;

He had a broad face and a

little round belly,

That shook, when he laughed, like a

bowlful of jelly.

He was chubby and plump,

a right jolly old elf,

And I laughed when I saw him,

in spite of myself;

A wink of his eye and a twist of his head,

Soon gave me to know

I had nothing to dread;

He spoke not a word, but went
straight to his work,
And filled all the stockings;
then turned with a jerk,
And laying his finger
aside of his nose,
And giving a nod, up the
chimney he rose;
He sprang to his sleigh,
to his team gave a whistle,
And away they all flew like
the down of a thistle.
But I heard him exclaim,
ere he drove out of sight,
'Happy Christmas to all,
and to all a good-night!'

PROFESSOR CLEMENT C MOORE,
'TWAS THE NIGHT BEFORE CHRISTMAS',
1822.

Father Christmas with Toys,
19th century. Hanson collection, Surrey.

Jolly Old
St Nicholas

Jolly old St Nicholas,
Lean your ear this way!
Don't you tell a single soul
What I'm going to say;
Christmas Eve is coming soon;
Now, you dear old man,
Whisper what you'll bring to me;
Tell me if you can.

When the clock is striking twelve,
When I'm fast asleep,
Down the chimney broad and black,
With your pack you'll creep;
All the stockings you will find
Hanging in a row;
Mine will be the shortest one,
You'll be sure to know.

Johnny wants a pair of skates;
Susy wants a dolly;
Nellie wants a story book;
She thinks dolls are folly;

As for me, my little brain
Isn't very bright;
Choose for me, old Santa Claus,
What you think is right.

ANON, TRADITIONAL AMERICAN CAROL.

Saint Nicholas, 1860. *Cut-out figure. Private collection.*

'The Children Give Presents'

On the evening before Christmas Day, one of the parlours is lighted up by the children, into which the parents must not go; a great yew bough is fastened on the table at a little distance from the wall, a multitude of little tapers are fixed in the bough, but not so as to burn it till they are nearly consumed, and coloured paper, etc, hangs and flutters from the twigs. Under this bough the children lay out in great order the presents they mean for their parents, still concealing in their pockets what they intend for each other. Then the parents are introduced, and each presents his little gift; they then bring out the remainder one by one, from their pockets, and present them with kisses and embraces.

SAMUEL TAYLOR COLERIDGE, 1798

The Arrival of the Christ-Child, 1896.
Wood engraving from a watercolour by A Brunner.
Archiv für Kunst und Geschichte, Berlin.

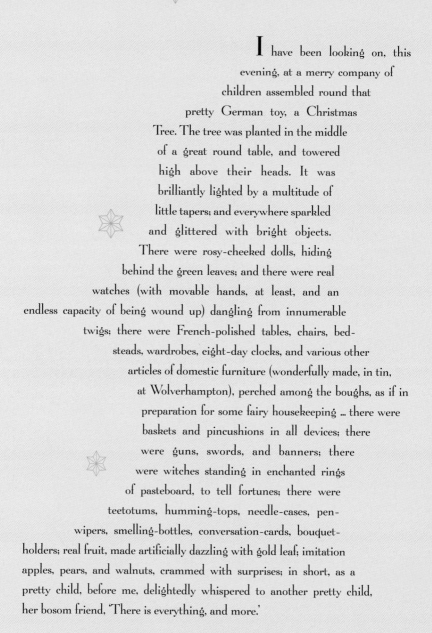

I have been looking on, this
evening, at a merry company of
children assembled round that
pretty German toy, a Christmas
Tree. The tree was planted in the middle
of a great round table, and towered
high above their heads. It was
brilliantly lighted by a multitude of
little tapers; and everywhere sparkled
and glittered with bright objects.
There were rosy-cheeked dolls, hiding
behind the green leaves; and there were real
watches (with movable hands, at least, and an
endless capacity of being wound up) dangling from innumerable
twigs; there were French-polished tables, chairs, bed-
steads, wardrobes, eight-day clocks, and various other
articles of domestic furniture (wonderfully made, in tin,
at Wolverhampton), perched among the boughs, as if in
preparation for some fairy housekeeping ... there were
baskets and pincushions in all devices; there
were guns, swords, and banners; there
were witches standing in enchanted rings
of pasteboard, to tell fortunes; there were
teetotums, humming-tops, needle-cases, pen-
wipers, smelling-bottles, conversation-cards, bouquet-
holders; real fruit, made artificially dazzling with gold leaf; imitation
apples, pears, and walnuts, crammed with surprises; in short, as a
pretty child, before me, delightedly whispered to another pretty child,
her bosom friend, 'There is everything, and more.'

CHARLES DICKENS, 'A CHRISTMAS TREE' IN CHRISTMAS STORIES, 1850.

Adam and Eve Decorating the Tree,
lithograph from a painting by Marie Wunsch, c 1895.

But now a knocking at the door
was heard, and such a rush immediately ensued that
she with laughing face and plundered dress was borne
towards it the centre of a flushed and boisterous
group, just in time to greet the father, who came home
attended by a man laden with Christmas toys and
presents. Then the shouting and the struggling, and
the onslaught that was made on the defenceless
porter! The scaling him with chairs for ladders, to dive
into his pockets, despoil him of brown-paper parcels,
hold on tight by his cravat, hug him round his neck,
pommel his back, and kick his legs in irrepressible

Christmas Morning,
engraving from a painting by
Viktor Carstens, painted in 1905.

affection! The shouts of wonder and delight with
which the development of every package was received!
The terrible announcement that the baby had been
taken in the act of putting a doll's frying-pan into his
mouth, and was more than suspected of having
swallowed a fictitious turkey, glued on a wooden
platter! The immense relief of finding this a false
alarm! The joy, and gratitude, and ecstasy! They are all
indescribable alike. It is enough that by degrees the
children and their emotions got out of the parlour, and
by one stair at a time, up to the top of the house;
where they went to bed, and so subsided.

CHARLES DICKENS, A CHRISTMAS CAROL, 1843.

Jo was the first to wake in the grey dawn of Christmas morning. No stockings hung at the fireplace, and for a moment she felt as much disappointed as she did long ago, when her little sock fell down because it was crammed so full of goodies. Then she remembered her mother's promise and, slipping her hand under her pillow, drew out a little crimson-covered book. She knew it very well, for it was that beautiful old story of the best life ever lived, and Jo felt that it was a true guidebook for any pilgrim going on a long journey. She woke Meg with a 'Merry Christmas', and bade her see what was under her pillow. A green-covered book appeared, with the same picture inside, and a few words written by their mother, which made their one present very precious in their eyes. Presently Beth and Amy woke to rummage and find their little books also, one dove-coloured, the other blue, and all sat looking at and talking about them, while the east grew rosy with the coming day.

LOUISA MAY ALCOTT, LITTLE WOMEN, 1868.

Gustave Doré, Christmas Eve, 1833–83. Louvre Museum, Paris.

At the Christmas Market

... one of those old German cities in
the hill country, when the streets and
the open places are covered with crisp
clean snow, and the mountains are
white with it ... The air is cold and
still, and heavy with the scent of the
Christmas-trees brought from the
forest for the pleasure of the children.
Day by day you see the rows of them
growing thinner, and if you go to the
market on Christmas Eve itself you
will find only a few trees left out in
the cold. The market is empty, the
peasants are harnessing their horses or
their oxen, the women are packing up
their unsold goods. In every home in
the city one of the trees that scented
the open air a week ago is shining now
with lights and little gilded nuts and
apples, and is helping to make that
Christmas smell, a compact of the pine
forest, wax candles, cakes and painted
toys, you must associate so long as you
live with Christmas in Germany.

MRS ALFRED SIDGWICK,
HOME LIFE IN GERMANY, 1908.

Franz Ignaz Pollinger, The First Christmas Tree
in Ried, 1848. Oil on canvas. Ethnology Museum, Ried.

John Latham, On the Evening of Christmas Eve, 1878. Lithograph. Library of Congress, Washington, DC.

Thursday, Christmas Eve, 1874

Writing Christmas letters all the morning.
In the afternoon I went to the Church with
Dora and Teddy to put up the Christmas
decorations. Dora has been busy for some
days past making the straw letters for the
Christmas text. Fair Rosamund and good
Elizabeth Knight came to the church to
help us and worked heartily and well.
They had made some pretty ivy knots
and bunches for the pulpit panels, and
the ivy blossoms, cleverly whitened with
flour, looked just like white flowers.

I took old John Bryant a Christmas
packet of tea and sugar and raisins from
my Mother. The old man had covered
himself almost entirely over in his bed to
keep himself warm, like a marmot in its
nest. He said, 'If I live till New Year's Day
I shall have seen ninety-six New Years.'
He said also, 'I do also see things flying
about me, thousands and thousands of
them about half the size of a large pea,
and they are red, white, blue and yellow
and all colours.' I asked Mr Morgan what
they were and he said they were the spirits
of just men made perfect.

REV FRANCIS KILVERT, KILVERT'S DIARY 1870–1879.

Twelfth Night

SIR TOBY, singing:

O! the twelfth day of December,–

MARIA.

– For the love o' God, peace!

Enter Malvolio.

MALVOLIO.

– My masters, are you mad? or what
  are you?
  Have you no wit, manners, nor honesty,
  but to gabble like tinkers at this time of night?
  Do ye make an alehouse of my lady's house,
  that ye squeak out your coziers' catches
  without any mitigation or remorse of voice?
  Is there no respect of place, persons, nor time,
  in you?

SIR TOBY.

We did keep time, sir, in our catches. Sneck up!

Pieter Brueghel the Younger, Winter, 1622–35. Oil on wood. National Art Museum, Bucharest.

MALVOLIO.

– Sir Toby, I must be round with you. My lady bade me
tell you, that, though she harbours you as her
kinsman, she's nothing allied to your disorders. If you
can separate yourself and your misdemeanours, you
are welcome to the house; if not, an it would please
you to take leave of her, she is very willing to bid you
farewell.

WILLIAM SHAKESPEARE, TWELFTH NIGHT, 2, III, 1607.

Adam and Eve and the Tree of Knowledge,
19th century. Painting. Private collection, Romania.

Adam
lay ybounden

Bounden in a bond;
Four thousand winter
Thought he not too long.

And all was for an apple,
An apple that he took,
As clerkes finden
Written in their book.

Ne had the apple taken been,
The apple taken been.
Ne had never our lady
A-been heavene queen.

Blessed be the time
That apple taken was,
Therefore we moun singen,
Deo, gracias!

15TH-CENTURY CAROL.

Hark how the bells,
Sweet silver bells,
All seem to say,
Throw cares away.

Christmas is here,
Bringing good cheer,
To young and old,
Meek and the bold.

Ding dong ding dong,
This is their song,
With joyful ring,
All carolling.

Oh how they pound,
Raising the sound,
O'er hill and dale,
Telling their tale.

Gaily they ring,
While people sing,
Songs of good cheer,
Christmas is here.

Merry, merry, merry, merry
Christmas,
Merry, merry, merry, merry Christmas,
On on they send,
On without end,
Their joyful tone to every home
Dong Ding dong ding, dong Bong.

'CAROL OF THE BELLS', A FAVOURITE
WITH UKRAINIAN AMERICANS.

Yvan Skolozdra, Three Children Dressed
as Kings Sing Carols, *20th century.*
Painting. Western Ukraine. The spirits of nature
can be seen in the trees, ready to join in the feast.

Festive Eating and Drinking

'e's got more to do than the ovens in England at Christmas-time.' The old Italian proverb underlines the prominent part that eating and drinking – often on a lavish scale – played in the English Christmas. The tradition goes back to feudal times, when the Great House in the village opened its doors to the local tenants and put on a massive dinner. The guests took their places in the great hall, seated strictly according to social rank. Then everyone stood up as the jester led in the Boar's Head, carried by the chief cook on a silver dish, followed by minstrels and servants bearing the other dishes. Slowly, the procession advanced on the high table, singing the Boar's Head carol:

The Boar's Head in hand bear I,

Bedeck'd with bays and rosemary;

And I pray you, my masters, be merry ...

In the royal palaces, the richness and abundance of the Christmas menu were staggering by today's standards. As well as the boar's head, delicacies included peacocks, capons, swan, pheasant, goose, beef, venison, spiced pies,

Christmas Trees.
Postcard, Musée des
Arts et Traditions
Populaires, Paris.

School of Fedoskino,
Nativity, 1993.
Painted egg.
Private collection.

salads, fricassees and custards. Another favourite was
frumenty, made of wheat boiled in milk with currants and
flavoured with nutmeg and cinnamon. Frumenty was served
with venison or fresh mutton, and in some areas was the first
thing people ate on Christmas morning.

In the 17th century, luxurious living and fragrant dishes were
abruptly thrown out by the Puritans:

> All plums the prophets' sons deny,
> And spice-broths are too hot,
> Treason's in a December pie,
> And death within the pot.

After the Restoration in 1660, the demands of the stomach
were once more richly attended to. A French visitor reported

with some wonder on the strange English passion for pies at Christmas: 'Every Family against Christmas makes a famous Pye, which they call Christmas Pye. It is a great Nostrum the Composition of this Pasty; it is a most learned Mixture of Neats-tongues, Chicken, Eggs, Sugar, Raisins, Lemon and Orange Peel, various kinds of Spicery, etc. They also make a Sort of Soup with Plums, which is not at all inferior to the Pye, which is in their language call'd Plum-porridge.'

★ ★ ★

At that time, no particular type of meat was favoured above the others. Only later did the turkey come to the fore, and became the great staple of Christmas dinner, along with Christmas pudding, a more solid descendant of plum-porridge made with raisins rather than plums. This is the traditional menu that later travelled with settlers to all parts of the world. In Australia, where the temperature may be 35°C, not everyone wants to eat hot food at midday, and many settle for a salad at the beach. When it gets a little cooler, some Australians go for a cold version of the traditional meal, laying out tasty seafood, glazed ham, cold chicken, duck or turkey and cold deli meats, followed by an ice dessert and extra treats such as mince pies, fruit cake and chocolates.

Many North American families eat their traditional stuffed turkey and pumpkin pie, but the people of the USA have such a rich blend of origins that regional variations abound. In Hawaii, they serve Turkey Teriyaki, made with a spicy marinade. In Baltimore, they eat sauerkraut with their turkey, and in other places the turkey is upstaged by, for example, the Creole Gumbo of Louisiana, a delicious mixture of ham, veal, chicken, shrimp, oysters and crabmeat. In New England they have Lumberjack Pie, a mashed potato crust filled with meats, onion and cinnamon.

★ ★ ★

In Europe, the pig supplied many traditional Christmas meals. Like the English with their boar's head, the Danes and the Swedes enjoyed their pig's head, while roast pork was a standing favourite in Germany, Romania and Serbia. In Catholic countries, the Vigil of the Nativity was a time for fasting, and no meat was allowed, hence the popularity in Italy of fish or stewed eels on Christmas Eve. Special loaves and cakes are a French speciality, with loaves in the shape of horns or a crescent and individual cakes representing animals and humans, and sometimes the Holy Child.

★ ★ ★

When the feasting was done, it was time for sports, games, dancing and other amusements. In many districts of England and Wales, neighbouring villages fought extremely vigorous football matches, with goals placed deep within each village. Some games were more like modern rugby. Men and women lined up together on each side as someone threw the ball high in the air, then the two sides piled into each other to try and capture the ball and rush back with it to their home goal.

Carl Larsson, Brita, 1901.

★ ★ ★

Another Christmas sport which seems to have a sacrificial origin was the hunting of small animals; squirrels and owls were sometimes the quarry, but more often it was the wren, one of the tiniest birds in Europe but also linked with legends of magical transformation. Elsewhere it was considered sacred, and the ritual act was performed so that the dead bird's feathers could be distributed round the village to provide protection in the coming year; later its body might be ceremoniously buried in the churchyard. Christmas was also a time for people to let their hair down and play games. Among the seasonal favourites were hunt the slipper, forfeits, bobbing for the apple and snap-dragon. This was often a game for Christmas Eve. A large dish was placed on a table and raisins or other dried fruit added to it. Brandy was poured over the raisins and set on fire. The lights in the room were all extinguished and then the company took turns to snatch raisins out of the fire. This was not at all easy to do unscathed, and the results produced howls of assorted laughter and pain. One of the most popular indoor games was blindman's buff. This was played all over Europe and known by various other names such as 'blind cow' and 'blind mouse', and may originally have derived from the custom of Christmas masking, mumming or disguising.

Masques were popular at the royal court, reaching their peak in the 16th and 17th centuries. The playwright Ben Jonson wrote a famous 'Masque of Christmas', for which the royal architect Inigo Jones designed the scenery. This had twelve principal characters. First to enter was Father Christmas, escorted by his guard and a drummer. Then came his ten children, led in by Cupid. They were followed by assorted characters such as the flamboyant Misrule wearing a great yellow ruff, Carol in a red cap and long coat, Minced Pie disguised as the cook's wife, and Gambol the tumbler with his hoop and bells. The company then danced about, exchanged their fairly fatuous lines and indulged in copious buffoonery to keep the audience happy.

Flag of the Mad
Mother Club of Dijon,
15th or 16th century.

At the local level, groups of mummers or masked players went round the towns and villages of Europe enacting plays during the winter festivals. They had the right to enter houses uninvited, where they launched into their repertoire, a medley of dance, song and drama. In the classic English play, the central figure is St George. He fights an infidel and one of them is killed. Then a doctor arrives and brings the dead man back to life. The plays have also been linked to the tradition of Christmas sword dancing found in Britain, Germany, Sweden, France and Italy. Here too a fight was mimed, followed by a violent death and the revival of the victim.

❖ ❖ ❖ Christmastide

LOVE CAME DOWN AT CHRISTMAS,

LOVE ALL LOVELY, LOVE DIVINE;

LOVE WAS BORN AT CHRISTMAS,

STAR AND ANGELS GAVE THE SIGN.

WORSHIP WE THE GODHEAD,

LOVE INCARNATE, LOVE DIVINE;

WORSHIP WE OUR JESUS:

BUT WHEREWITH FOR SACRED SIGN?

LOVE SHALL BE OUR TOKEN,

LOVE BE YOURS AND LOVE BE MINE,

LOVE TO GOD AND ALL MEN,

LOVE FOR PLEA AND GIFT AND SIGN.

CHRISTINA ROSSETTI, 1830–94.

Russian art, Nativity, leaves added to the psalter of Egbert, Bishop of Trier.

National Archaeological Museum, Cividale-Del-Friuli.

 **The**

last day before Christmas was over. Night had come, a bright winter's night. The stars came out. The moon rose majestically in the sky, lighting the good people and the world all around, so that everyone could enjoy singing carols beneath the windows and glorifying Christ. The cold was sharper than it had been in the morning, but it was so quiet that you could hear snow crunching under people's boots a mile away. None of the boys' groups had yet appeared beneath the windows; only the moon slipped in a surreptitious glance now and again, as though to encourage the girls, who were still getting ready, to hurry up and venture out on the crunchy snow. Just at that moment, wreaths of smoke spurted from a chimney and rose into the sky like a cloud, and with them appeared a witch, riding on her broomstick.

GOGOL, 'CHRISTMAS EVE', 1831.

V E *Starkova, School of Mstiora, Christmas Eve,* 1979. *Box-lid. Private collection.*

Christmas Day

Three masses every priest doth sing
Upon that solemn day,

With offerings unto every one,
That so the more may play.

This done, a wooden childe in clowtes
Is on the altar set,

About the which both boys and gyrles
Do dance and trimly jet;

And Carols sing in praise of Christ,
And, for to help them heare,

The organs answere every verse
With sweet and solemn cheere.

The priests do rore aloude, and round
About the parentes stande,

To see the sport, and with their voyce
Do helpe them and their bande.

CHRISTMAS DAY DEVOTIONS, 16TH CENTURY.

Man disguised as a goat, illustration for Le Roman d'Alexandre,
14th century. The Bodleian Library, Oxford.

Soul! soul! for a soul-cake!

I pray, good missis, a soul-cake!

An apple or pear, a plum or a cherry,

Any good thing to make us merry.

One for Peter, two for Paul,

Three for Him who made us all.

Up with the kettle, and down with the pan,

Give us good alms, and we'll be gone.

TRADITIONAL WASSAILING SONG, SHROPSHIRE, ENGLAND.

CHRISTMAS WITH
SIR ROGER

Sir Roger, after the laudable Custom of his Ancestors, always keeps open House at Christmas. I learned from him that he had killed eight Fat Hogs for this Season, and that he had sent a String of Hogs'-puddings with a Pack of Cards to every poor Family in the Parish. I have often thought, says Sir Roger, it happens very well that Christmas should fall out in the Middle of Winter. It is the most dead uncomfortable Time of the Year, when the poor People would suffer very much from their Poverty and Cold, if they had not good Chear, warm Fires, and Christmas Gambols to support them. I love to rejoice their poor Hearts at this Season, and to see the whole Village in my great Hall. I allow a double Quantity of Malt to my Small Beer, and set it running for twelve Days to every one that calls for it. I always have a piece of Cold Beef and Mince-pye on the Table, and am wonderfully pleased to see my Tenants pass away a whole Evening in playing their innocent Tricks ...

JOSEPH ADDISON, 1672–1719, TALES OF
SIR ROGER DE COVERLEY FROM THE SPECTATOR.

Carl Larsson, Christmas Eve, 1904–6. Watercolour from Larsson's book Spadarfvet.

Noel is leaving us,
Sad 'tis to tell,
But he will come again,
Adieu, Noel.

His wife and his children
Weep as they go;
On a grey horse
They ride thro' the snow.

The Kings ride away
In the snow and the rain,
After twelve months
We shall see them again.

EPIPHANY SONG.

Ludwig Richter, Christ Night, 1855. Drawing with watercolour.
Staatliches Kupferstichkabinett, Dresden.

Bibliography

26–27: The Gospel according to St Luke, 2, 1–20, The Holy Bible, Authorised Version, 1611.

30–31: The Gospel according to St Matthew, 1, 18–25; 2, 1–12, The Holy Bible, Authorised Version, 1611.

32: The Book of James or Protevangelium, 19.1–20.3, The Apocryphal New Testament, translated by M R James, 1924.

34: 'How the Ass and the Ox Came to the Crib', adapted from a traditional folk tale. Various sources.

36: 'O Come All Ye Faithful', John Francis Wade, c 1743. Traditional hymn. Various sources.

38: 'Long, Long, Ago', Anon, traditional Christmas poem. Various sources.

40: Robert Southwell, c 1561–95, 'Weigh not His crib, His wooden dish' in 'New Prince, New Pomp'. Collected Poems.

43: New Zealand carol, 'No touch of winter's frosty breath'. Quoted in T G Crippen, Christmas and Christmas Lore, London and Glasgow, 1929.

45: 'Hark! the Herald Angels Sing', Charles Wesley, 1739. Hymns Ancient and Modern, 1861.

46: Christina Rossetti, 1839–94, 'What Can I Give Him (Give My Heart)' in 'A Christmas Carol'. Collected Poems.

49: 'Once in Royal David's City', Cecil Francis Alexander, 1848. Hymns Ancient and Modern, 1861.

50: John Keble, poem 'Christmas Day' from The Christian Year, 1827. Various sources.

52: Jacobus de Voragine, The Golden Legend, 1261–66.

56: 'We Three Kings of Orient Are', John Henry Hopkins, Jr, 1857. Carol. Various sources.

59: Hymn of St Anatolius, 5th century, in R F Littledale, Offices from the Service Books of the Holy Eastern Church, London, 1863.

60: Dialogue between Herod and the Three Wise Men, medieval carol from Thuringia, Germany, translated in Karl Hase, Miracle Plays and Sacred Dramas, London, 1880.

62: Nahum Tate, 'While Shepherds Watched (their Flocks by Night)', 1700. Hymns Ancient and Modern, 1861.

72: 'A Virgin most pure', traditional carol, Anon, pre-1734. Various sources.

75: 'Whom saw ye, O shepherds?' Responsory for Christmas Matins.

76: 'Away in a Manger', traditional carol. Various sources.

79: Mme Th Bentzon, 'Christmas in France' in The Century Magazine, New York, 1901.

80: Richard Crashaw, 'In the Holy Nativity of our Lord', 1646, poem collected in Carmen Deo Nostro, 1652.

82: W H D Rouse, 'Religious Tableaux in Italian Churches' in Folk-Lore, Vol V, London, 1894.

85: Epiphany play from Rouen in E Du Méril, Origines latines du théâtre moderne, Paris, 1849, quoted in Clement A Miles, Christmas in Ritual and Tradition, London, 1912.

86: St Bridget of Sweden, 1303–73, Revelations, published 1492.

88: Adapted from Thomas of Celano, Lives of St Francis, c 1248.

96: Jacobus de Voragine, The Golden Legend, 1275. 'Englished' by William Caxton, 1483.

100: Horatio Alger, 1832–99, 'St Nicholas'. Various sources.

102–105: Professor Clement C Moore, 'A Visit from St Nicholas', 1822. Various sources.

106: 'Jolly Old St Nicholas', carol, Anon. Various sources.

108: Samuel Taylor Coleridge, The Friend, 1798.

110: Charles Dickens, 'A Christmas Tree' in Christmas Stories, London, 1850.

112–113: Charles Dickens, A Christmas Carol, London, 1843.

114: Louisa May Alcott, Little Women, 1868.

116: Mrs Alfred Sidgwick, Home Life in Germany, London, 1908.

119: Rev Francis Kilvert, Kilvert's Diary 1870–79.

120–121: William Shakespeare, Twelfth Night, 2, III, 1607. Various sources.

123: 'Adam lay ybounden', carol, Anon, 15th century. Various sources.

124: 'Carol of the Bells', traditional carol, Anon. Various sources.

132: Christina Rossetti, 1830–94, 'Christmastide'. Collected Poems.

134: Gogol, 'Christmas Eve' in Evenings in the Village, 1831–2.

136: Christmas Day devotions in Thomas Naogeorgus, The Popish Kingdome, 1553, translated by Barnabe Googe, 1570, published London, 1880.

137: Traditional wassailing song from Shropshire, England.

138: Joseph Addison, 1672–1719, tales of Sir Roger de Coverley from The Spectator.

140: 'Noel is leaving us', French Epiphany song, translated by Rev R L Gales, The Nation, London, 1910.

Picture Credits

Acknowledgments

This highly illustrated work drawing on many sources was for me a pleasure and also a test. The testing part was having to overcome my feelings of frustration when faced with such a choice of wonderful and moving words and images. Such an abundant parade of myths, legends, poems, paintings and sculptures from every century, all devoted to the holy days of Christmas.

This book was also a chance for me to test the firmness of friendships formed during my time in Paris. I am most grateful to all of them. Monelle and Simon Diner offered, with characteristic generosity, photographs of magnificent works painted on lacquer, which they love so much. Edouard de Lumley, an acknowledged connoisseur of Ukrainian culture, also went to much trouble to introduce me to the popular traditions of that country. Iléana Gaïta, a colleague and friend, translated with great talent and skill the two popular Romanian songs featured here. Yves Benoît and Mesdames and Messieurs Prochalski, Thomsen, Stoll and Niola gave up their time to provide me with original documents and to improve the translations of texts I had chosen.

Bernard Dupaigne, Nancy Wise, Lionel Gauthier and Liliane Marçol gave me much encouragement, while Gaia Ficher, my young collaborator, helped me with my researches. Finally, Tatiana Benfougal, true to form, was most generous with her accounts of Slavic culture.

I thank them all, and hope that they, like everyone else on earth, may fully enjoy celebrating the Nativity, symbolically re-enacted each year, the pleasures of the New Year, and universal peace.

Yvonne de Sike
Paris, 2001

First published by Hazan, an imprint of Hachette-Livre
43 Quai de Grenelle, Paris 75905, Cedex 15, France
© 2001
Under the title Les Dits de Noël
All rights reserved

English language translation produced by Translate-A-Book, Oxford
English Language adaptation prepared by Michael Leitch

© 2003 English translation, Octopus Publishing Group Ltd, London
This edition published by Hachette Illustrated UK, Octopus Publishing Group,
2–4 Heron Quays, London, E14 4JP

Editorial manager: Hélène de Bettignies, assisted by Elodie Fondacci
Design and layout: Sylvie Millet
Reproduction: Arts Graphiques du Centre, Saint-Avertin
Printed and bound in Singapore by Tien Wah Press Ltd
ISBN: 1-84430-016-1